Work and Play in Early Childhood

Freya Jaffke

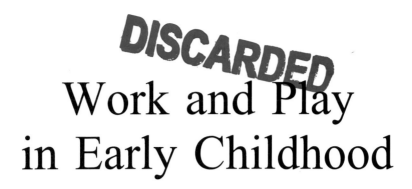

Work and Play
in Early Childhood

Freya Jaffke

Translated by Christian von Arnim

Anthroposophic Press

First published in German under the title
Spielen und arbeiten im Waldorfkindergarten
by Verlag Freies Geistesleben in 1991
First published in English in 1996 by Floris Books
and in the United States by Anthroposophic Press, Inc
Hudson, NY 12534   www.anthropress.org
Reprinted in 2000

10 9 8 7 6 5 4 3 2

ISBN 0-88010-442-2

Printed in the Netherlands

Contents

Foreword

The examples referred to in this study of the development and education of children during the first seven years of life are based on lectures which were delivered within the framework of the International Association of Waldorf Kindergartens.

All accounts are based on observations and experience gained over decades working in the Waldorf kindergarten in Reutlingen, Germany. It is hoped that parents and educators faced with the task of bringing up small children will find inspiration here to help them in their daily endeavours. This perspective on the distinct character of children may enable parents and educators to find their individual way, as is appropriate to circumstances and particular abilities.

The first chapter gives an overview of the different developmental stages of the child and offers thoughts on the ways adults can participate in play situations. The following chapter gives an insight into daily life in the kindergarten. It also contains observations and thoughts on the way small children will, quite naturally and independently reach for a needle and thread when they see adults sewing, for example.

The final two chapters deal with the extent to which small children still require the careful creation of a protective 'mantle,' a warmly enveloping environment for their development, which still allows them the greatest possible freedom within which to unfold the forces of their will.

All the experiences reported here are based on Rudolf Steiner's study of the human being. This study offers us a source of security and great pleasure in our daily encounters with children.

1

Stages of development
in early childhood

Tasks and objectives for
parents and educators

Anyone wishing to understand children during their first seven years of life will have to observe the individual stages of their development very carefully. Before doing so, it is useful to look at the overall situation of children at the beginning of their lives.

At the birth of a child the parents provide the body from two hereditary streams. The body is united with a being consisting of soul and spirit, which makes up the human individual.

Despite its external perfection, the physical body is in many respects still incomplete: the internal organs have not yet taken on their distinct forms; movement is still unspecific, chaotic and arbitrary; the nervous and sensory sphere of the body is dominated by a great openness.

During their first six to seven years children have to take hold of their body from within and give it the kind of distinct structure which causes it to become a useful 'instrument' once the process of organ formation is concluded. Once further developmental stages have been achieved, the body will provide

A three-and-a-half-year-old carefully places one block of wood next to another but without any particular purpose in mind; he simply continues building until the basket is empty.

the instrument through which the soul and spirit of the individual can be revealed, with the body causing as little hindrance as possible.

We are able to observe the process by which individuals connect themselves with their bodies. For example, we can see how small children strive gradually to regulate the arbitrary movements of their legs and arms, to acquire upright posture and, in learning to walk, to take part in the relationship of balance and equilibrium in the world. We can observe how small children gradually progress from the universal language of gurgles to the precise language sounds of their environment, increasing their powers of articulation all the time. We can also see how the clumsy actions of early childhood turn into more distinct, purposeful activity.

Throughout these processes we can still observe the individual personality and its effort to infiltrate the body and make it its own. This internal process of taking on form is closely bound up with the external impressions confronting the child from the immediate surroundings.

Small children, unprotected, are at the mercy of their immediate environment. Their whole body acts as a single sensory organ unselfconsciously uniting external impressions with the child's internal world, functioning in a similar way to the eyes. Eyes themselves do not see. They act as mediators through which *we* see. Likewise, the child's body acts as a sensory organ for the individual, the soul and spiritual being.

This interaction of external impressions with the child's internal organic development is revealed in the wonderful power of imitation with which every healthy child is born. Every perception is first deeply assimilated, then grasped with the will and reflected back to the outside in echo-like activity.

Two important priorities therefore arise for parents and educators. The first is concerned with protection. As far as possible we should carefully select the impressions which confront and surround the children.

It is fine for children to be surrounded by happy family sounds, chatting, singing and so on, but they should not be subjected to noise and quarrelling. They should be protected from artificial noise such as radio, television, hi-fi, and so on. The use of a single delicate colour for cradle canopies and nursery wallpaper has a more calming effect than bright patterns, even if the latter look as if they might appeal more to children. If children are taken shopping it is better for them to be able to face their parent rather than being subjected to the distraction and bustle of the street.

The second major priority consists of guiding children gently into life, by allowing them to learn from life for life. The most useful and helpful way of doing this is by exploiting the child's inborn ability to imitate, rather than by teaching clever things. This requires that we, as adults, make an effort to be good human 'role models' encouraging impulses in children through our actions. We cannot teach children the power of imitation as it is bound up with the will and has to be grasped by the will of each individual child. However, we can become aware of our own behaviour: of the way in which we go about our work in the home and the garden; the way in which we address other people; the way in which we take care of others; and the way in which we build and develop our environment. Children observe all this, and assimilate their observations so that they become involved in the processes which govern the development of the body. Unable to distinguish between rational and irrational actions, children model their behaviour on the examples they see around them. Anyone interacting with a child therefore becomes part of the educational process for that child.

In the first six to seven years of life, the imitative behaviour

Five and six-year-olds purposefully plan and build pathways for their trains.

of children passes through three distinct phases. The capacity for imitation is connected with the forces of organic development which influence the whole body, starting at the head and reaching to the tips of the toes. Although these forces run through the whole body, during the first stage, (from birth to approximately two and a half years), they are concentrated in the development of the organs of the nervous and sensory system. During this time children acquire three of the most important human abilities: the ability to counter the force of gravity by standing upright and walking; the ability to speak; and with the advent of speech, the ability to think in words. Children learn these skills entirely through imitation. Tragic examples in history have shown that children who grow up exclusively in the company of animals do not acquire these human abilities. This clearly demonstrates that human behaviour can only be learnt from humans.

From the age of crawling to the 'terrible twos'

What do children do in this first stage of their lives?

They have only just become mobile through crawling or walking, when they begin to investigate everything and cause havoc in their immediate home environment. They follow their mother around and want to do everything she does. They love banging saucepans lids and spoons; they stick their hands into the wash-basin, pull out things and put them back in again, spilling water all over the place; they push the broom around but distribute the dirt everywhere; they remove things which have just been put in the right place and eagerly put them somewhere else. Everything is done with the sense of 'Me too.' They love moving and handling things, especially real household appliances, and they have no insight into the meaning and purpose of what their mother or the other adults around them are doing. In such circumstances, adults can only manage to do their work slowly. They would finish their tasks much more quickly without such willing 'assistance,' but by having their children with them while they work they have not just dealt with the housework or gardening, they have carried out educational work at the same time. This realization should play a much greater part in our awareness of the process of education today.

As well as interacting enthusiastically with their surroundings, there are also moments when children want to stay close to their mothers and watch attentively as an apple is peeled or a needle threaded. They may wish to absorb themselves by filling and emptying a basket, building towers in order to knock them down again, or pushing the doll's pram around as they sing a song. It is therefore important that we consider carefully the type of toys our children play with. The best kind of toys are those which occur naturally in the outside world, or which can easily be made by hand.[1] The natural organic forms of such toys will make an impression on children and stimulate their inner processes of organic development. 'Toys with dead, mathematical forms alone, have a desolating and killing effect upon the formative forces of the child.'[2]

Children go through their first real crisis period when their sense of self begins to develop. This often happens between their second and third birthdays and is therefore sometimes referred to as the 'terrible twos.' Children of this age are increasingly aware of their own will but they have to learn to create a harmonious relationship between their will and their surroundings. Whereas they previously entered into everything in the spirit of 'Me too,' their overwhelming feeling now is 'But I don't want to.'

Between the ages of three and five

Let us now turn to the second stage, the time between the ages of three and five.

The formative life forces which were active mainly in the region of the head, now work mainly in the middle part of the body. This is where the rhythmical organs, the heart and lungs, are found. During this period, two completely new faculties appear in the child and these illustrate the child's new relationship to the surroundings. These faculties are the imagination and the memory.

Here are some examples taken from the way healthily developed children play:

A four-year-old boy places lots of small round wooden blocks in front of him on the table and asks me: 'Do you want mineral water, beer or apple juice?'

A four-year-old girl takes a piece of bark, places two stones on it and says: 'I've got a ship with two sailors.' She then approaches me and asks: 'I've brought you some chocolate, do you want it?' and puts the stones down in front of me. The piece of bark then turns into a roof for a little house for gnomes.

A footstool starts off as a doll's cooker, turns on its side to become a manger and then is turned over completely to become first a doll's bed and then part of a train.

These examples show how children at this age are capable of transforming things from their surroundings, using them in a way which is quite different from their original purpose and, with the help of their imagination, creating something new. Children see an object, remember something — perhaps only distantly — and their imagination does the rest. In order to do this they need to have seen or experienced such things already.

Children can only recreate ships as they play if they have seen a ship before, even if only in a picture book.

A characteristic of play at this age is that it is stimulated by external circumstances. This is why it is important that there are objects available to children in their immediate environment which can be transformed by them. It is also important that these objects are not completed, enabling children to use their imagination to transform what they have around them into something they have seen previously. Everything depends on the inner work. 'As the muscles of the hand grow firm and strong in performing the work for which they are fitted, so the brain and other organs of the physical body of man are guided into the right lines of development if they receive the right impressions from the environment.'[3]

It also becomes clear that the way children play is very varied. Daily events are copied, but frequently — often without any apparent connection — they change spontaneously. Children think of something new all the time. Some adults might despair at this and think that their children are unable to play in any concentrated manner. But the very continuity of the way children of this age play involves concentration. Admittedly, this type of play can create a fair amount of chaos, but it can be described as meaningful chaos because it always has a creative effect. Once children have passed the age of five a natural change occurs. Adults can allow a sufficient time for tidying up once the children have finished playing and can set an example by joining in themselves. In this way cleaning up becomes a familiar and enjoyable routine rather than a lonely chore.

Between the ages of five and seven

The third great developmental step of the first seven years begins around the age of five. The forces of organic development in the rhythmical realm begin to relax and they now begin to concentrate their work in the sphere of the limbs and the metabolism. At this stage children become increasingly skilful and dextrous.

Many children — particularly those who had been able to play comprehensively and creatively — pass through a second crisis at the age of five. They experience real boredom for the first time. They come to you and say: 'I don't know what to do.' It is as if they have been abandoned by their imagination and are suddenly bereft of ideas. There is no point appealing to the children's imagination, reminding them of how happily they used to play. In fact their imagination needs to be protected. They should be encouraged to participate to a greater extent in what the adults around them are doing, for instance peeling apples, drying up, sweeping, baking, sewing. After a while — it might only be a matter of days — new ideas for play will arise naturally in the children. A transformation has taken place. The stimulus for play comes less from external objects and more from within the children. Children of this age have an inner picture, an image in their mind of past events and they can make use of this in their play, independently of place and time and people.

Five- and six-year-old children like to huddle together, tell each other things and plan their play. They might for example build a café in which folded cloths become napkins, menus and aprons. Or they might set up a cold buffet in which little toy sheep are offered as fish. A drinks vendor might sit behind the large log with several branches from which he can pull every kind of drink.

On another occasion they might set up a doctor's surgery with needles, stethoscopes, bandages and a waiting room in which the folded cloths now turn into magazines.

Other typical subjects for play might be a garbage truck, ambulance with a flashing light, a school, a joinery workshop, a fire engine, a cable railway, a telephone exchange, a deep sea diving station, and so on. Play is more and more organized, although it is still possible for it suddenly to change in midstream, when someone has a brilliant idea.

Rather than requiring new and sophisticated toys, children of this age need familiar things around them. As they grow older they will regard these things differently. Before the age of five ideas are sparked off by objects, whereas after the age of five the initial idea comes first, followed by the attempt to find the appropriate materials. This is where the imagination is set to work again.

It can no longer be taken for granted that all children can play with the spontaneity, fulfilment and enthusiasm appropriate to their stage of development. This is probably due less to the children themselves than to the great barrage of influences to which they are subjected from the beginning of childhood. Ready-made, technically sophisticated toys can make it difficult for children to be satisfied with apparently unsophisticated things such as natural materials, pieces of cloth, twigs from trees, and so on. Healthy children want to be at the centre of the process of play rather than simply observing specific gadgets and sophisticated technological equipment. The fascination with this soon passes, leaving behind a feeling of emptiness and the demand for more.

It is really important therefore, to create spaces — at home and in the kindergarten — which allow children to play creatively. Most importantly this should include the opportunity for imitation. This is best achieved by the presence of adults, happily and purposefully occupied, accompanying the children quietly as they play. A calm, happy creative atmosphere is much more important than clever words and instructions to the children about what to play. Children should be 'securely enveloped' by the adults' work, and included in it as much as possible even if they are not participating in it directly. That appears to be a contradiction, but can be experienced by any parent who is involved in projects around the house or garden, or who sits down in the playroom with a sewing basket or ironing board, radiating calmness and interest. The adults who surround children are extremely important as they provide a rhythmical and ordered structure for the children. They can demonstrate an enjoyment of work as well as the willingness to work hard. Such efforts are never wasted as small children are natural imitators!

The reward for such hard work lies in the fact that children who have been cared for in this way will be able to play happily and contentedly, building secure foundations for their future happiness.

So the objectives facing all those responsible for the care and education of children are clear. In the early years of childhood children must be allowed to experience and embrace the individual stages of their development. The challenges these different stages offer allow them to strengthen and practise their skills and powers, so that when their bodies are fully formed and ready to undergo their first transformation children can approach the challenge of school positively, and with the confidence to feel that they are equal to the demands which they will encounter there.

2

Life and work in a Waldorf kindergarten

Life in the kindergarten can be compared to living and working in a large family. The group of children comprises on average twenty boys and girls between the ages of three and seven. The teachers ensure that the day is rhythmically structured and ordered, balancing caring for the house and its contents with handicrafts and creative activities. These are supplemented by activities connected with specific times of the year, and leading into the celebration of festivals.

The rhythmical structure of the day

Before describing in detail the various types of work, in the kindergarten, we shall look at the typical course of a day and the way time is divided up.

All the members of staff come together for a brief meeting half an hour before the main school begins. Then the kindergarten opens so that parents can bring older brothers and sisters to school at the same time. There is free play for a good hour with the children themselves deciding what they want to play. They might gather in small groups in the dolls' area or the building corner for example, to build houses or play fire engines or fishing boats. Some might join in with what the adults are doing. The smallest ones might play by themselves

Four and five-year-olds build a landscape for gnomes and stand-up dolls in order subsequently to use it to act out a story.

or they might be included by the bigger ones' games, for example, as patients in medical practice, guests at a doll's birthday party or 'children' at a make-believe school. Some smaller ones might prefer to sit close to an adult at first, before starting to play.

At the end of playtime, the adults begin by tidying up their work place, putting tools and other equipment back in their place. Sometimes the floor will need to be swept. This heralds a general period of tidying up in which the children can participate in a number of ways depending on their age. Once this is finished, they all go to the toilet and wash their hands. The ones who are back first begin to lay the tables for a morning snack, with spoons, place mats and vases of flowers. Before starting to eat, everyone gathers for some simple rhythmical games, based on songs and poems, appropriate to the time of year. The adult sings the song or recites the poem accompanied by calm movements which the children can follow and copy.

Everyone settles down together to eat breakfast, which will have been prepared beforehand. The food is different for each day of the week. It might be home-baked honey-and-salt bread, millet porridge, wheat meal porridge, muesli or wheat grain and wholemeal rolls. These will be accompanied by herb tea and fruit depending on the time of the year.

After breakfast there is a second period of free play for another hour. This might take place in the garden where there is a choice of the sand pit, buckets and spades, skipping ropes, balls, wheel barrows, shovels and rakes. If it is too cold to play outside we go to the nearby park for a walk with plenty of games involving running and catching, to keep everyone warm.

About half an hour before kindergarten finishes, when everything has been put away again, shoes have been changed and hands washed, all the children — some cradling dolls in their arms — gather in the story corner to hear a fairy tale. The same fairy tale is repeated over several days.

The story concludes the morning activities and the children are then collected at lunch time. Some kindergartens also run afternoon groups, lasting until four or five o'clock.

If we reflect on the day which has just been described, we can see that it is divided into two great 'breaths.' During the period of free play the children are able 'breathe out' fully, in that they are free to follow their own impulses. The time devoted to rhythmical play and breakfast on the other hand is a kind of 'breathing in,' in other words joining in a common activity. The second period of free play is another time for 'breathing out' again, the fairy tale period for 'breathing in.' The 'breathing out' periods are very long, to accommodate the needs of small children but they balance the short 'breathing in' periods.

Different artistic activities all have their place on respective days within the week, for example, painting with water colours during free play, eurythmy in place of the rhythmical games, modelling with beeswax during the winter months in place of the fairy tale. The last day of the week is always the day for cleaning the tables and shelves and polishing them.

The artistic activities do not in any way interrupt the children's free play. This is never curtailed. On a painting day, for instance, the children can have a go at painting for as long or short a time as they want to. They decide for themselves when they want to start or stop an activity.

Six to seven-year-olds move heavy logs up and down the steps using their 'situational intelligence.'

What the adults do and make

Various tasks arise for the adults during the course of the kindergarten day. These mainly include preparing breakfast for the children, caring for the room (for example, arranging flowers, dusting, keeping the seasons corner in order) and preparing for the festivals.

Toys must also be made and cared for. Most are home-made, sewn, carved, knotted or woven from cane, and some may need to be repaired or washed and ironed. Because of all the different things they might need, the adults have to arrange their work places carefully so that they do not continually have to go and fetch things. Sewing (see p. 31) and carving can serve as examples for closer examination.

Carpentry

Carving spoons and little bowls for the dolls' corner, human and animal figures, parts for trains, candle sticks and so on, is extraordinarily satisfying work. If the adults have sufficient experience, they can easily undertake this kind of work with small children around. The children then have the opportunity to see how things which they will later be allowed to use are created. They experience unconsciously the amount of effort and work required to finish an object and their approach to it becomes quite different. They can also imitate the hard work, joy and intensity which went into making the object.

Children will always gaze on in amazement when different tools from the tool cupboard, saws, planes, chisels and so on, are used on the work bench. Leftover wood is always much in demand by the children. They use it to build things or they sandpaper it smooth in the 'workshop.' Wood shavings are collected and might be used to decorate a chestnut cake or as food for the horses or for cooking by a doll, to name just a few ideas. The carpenter must definitely be invited for a meal at the beautifully laid table to join in a dolls' birthday party when the candles will be lit. The children follow the progress of the carpenter's work from one day to the next, running their hands over the carved surfaces and sharing the joy when such a piece of work has been completed and is ready for waxing and polishing.

Children imitate the carpenter in their own way by 'carving' bark or rotten wood with small sticks. Obviously they are not given knives, but they are allowed to use small saws. They carry out their work for a period of at least one week and probably for several. This is of great benefit for the children. Every day when they arrive they encounter the continuity of the workshop atmosphere — just as they did yesterday and will do tomorrow. This gives the children a deep sense of security which grows with them and which gives them a calm sense of assurance.

Because the children learn that we produce almost all our toys ourselves, they develop an attitude of self-sufficiency, a sense that what we need we can make ourselves. This encourages them to become less demanding, and in appreciating and respecting things, they become creative and skilful themselves.

While the activities of the adults in kindergarten are determined by their own particular skills, this does not mean that they do not try to acquire new skills. However, there will be a particular focus in the work of each individual kindergarten, such as a particular type of embroidery, wood carving, plant dye, basket weaving, reflecting the particular skills of the adults who work there.

Preparing festivals

Another area of kindergarten work lies in preparing the festivals.

The great sources of inspiration which guide activities in the kindergarten are, on the one hand, the developing small child and, on the other hand, the cycle of the year. Small children still have an intimate relationship with their surroundings, and this is something which should be cultivated. All our activities are therefore suffused with the events of the seasons, from year to year. The older children expect the same activities to recur each year, and they begin to feel the joy of anticipation of the festivals as they come round. Discussion of the meaning and significance of the festivals is largely reserved for a later stage of development. In the first instance the young children are simply given the opportunity to feel and assimilate the meaning which lies in doing things. This impresses itself deeply on the life and growth forces of young children.

Autumn, and the harvest festival are a good example of this.

To begin with, we take a sheaf of different kinds of grain. The stalks are shortened and the ears tied together into a large harvest wreath. For days the children sit among a mountain of straw. Some cut the stalks, others make straw bundles or stick lots of short stalks together to make a long 'fishing rod.' Others assemble small bunches of ears which they give to an adult to bind together. A good part of the straw is collected together and kept for the winter when the rose bushes need to be protected or the bird house needs a new roof. The rest of the straw is then burned jubilantly at the bonfire.

Then we take ears of wheat and thresh them over a number of days. The corn is gathered together and, with a great deal of effort, ground into fine meal using a handmill. This is then used to bake bread for the harvest festival.

We have used this time to collect and bring back the treasures which are so richly available in autumn. We have gathered fallen apples and made them into purée, dried apple rings and herbs. We have collected acorns, chestnuts, rosehips, beechnuts and coloured leaves on our walks.

The harvest festival

Parents are invited to the harvest festival. All the children bring along a small basket containing a small piece of fruit or a vegetable from the garden, or something they have found on a walk. They place these on the harvest table which has been specially prepared for the occasion. A large loaf of bread sits in the middle of the table, surrounded by flowers, ears of corn and candles.

At the beginning of the ceremony everyone performs the harvest dance together. This will have been practised in the preceding weeks. Then everyone sits down at the harvest table, we light the candles, say grace and then divide up the second large loaf which we have baked. Honey-and-salt bread has to be particularly well chewed so we all sit quietly together and tuck in. Afterwards each child hands over their piece of fruit. These are cut into pieces and distributed round the table. After the candles have been extinguished, everyone rushes out to the bonfire where some of the parents are looking after the baked potatoes. Once the potatoes have been eaten, the festival is concluded with every child being given a small harvest posy made up of the various types of grain.

This festival is the climax of our harvest thanksgiving, but there is gratitude in all our gestures during the weeks of preparation.

If we look back we can see that all work in the kindergarten was done in such a way that the children could participate in it. They could join in and imitate, or, in the midst of the activities, following their own inclination without anyone being bothered by this. They were interested in the work going on around them and were content to be enveloped by it. Because the various activities come around every year, the children gradually learn to place them in the context of the year, and as they grow older, they have experience of the same activities differently each year.

Rhythm and repetition: Example and imitation

To summarize, the education of small children is based on two very important aspects. One of these is rhythm and repetition. The activities the children engage in are completely bound up with the seasons of the year. The teachers help the children to develop an increasingly deep and living relationship with the events of the year in many different ways. As well as the seasons themselves this also includes a deeper understanding of the Christian festivals as they occur throughout the year. Observing the seasons and festivals each year offers children a wealth of activities and experiences without the pressure of questions which require reflection or feats of memory. Great importance is attached to the establishment of a happy, normal creative atmosphere in which, unbeknown to the children, the seeds of reverence and gratitude are being sown.

The second important aspect for the education of small children is that of role modelling and imitation. Since adults provide a model for the children until they begin school, they need to be particularly concerned with self-education.

All normally developing children receive their guidance and their impulses for their actions, their play and behaviour from the adult world. In going about their work teachers are aware of each individual child in their care. The children are left quite free to imitate. All of them may emulate the adult in their own time and in their own way as they complete their learning stages. If the adult activity around them is sufficiently broad and if it is repeated often enough, all children will find what they are unconsciously seeking for the stages of their development, in relation to their own imitative capacity.

− 3 −

Handwork in the kindergarten

When we talk about 'handwork' in the Waldorf kindergarten, we mean a great variety of happy, imitative activities. It is not necessary to think of all kinds of different activities which might improve the children's dexterity, and then make them carry out these activities. If children are allowed to watch adults making things to prepare for the festivals, for example, sewing, darning, mending or doing embroidery, they will quickly start wanting to work with the same kind of equipment and materials. Children like nothing better than to work with the same things as adults. It is therefore an excellent idea to put all the left-overs from craft work (bits of material, felt, pieces of fur, coloured paper and anything else) into a special basket from which the children can help themselves at any time.

It is important that children should be free to work according to their own abilities and ideas. In situations where insurmountable difficulties arise, for example if they cannot quite manage the scissors, the thread simply will not go through the eye of the needle, or the thread needs a knot at the end, we can give unobtrusive assistance.

The activity is much more important for the child than the produce. This is because when they make something according to their own will they make use of what is readily available — the tools — so they are unconsciously exercising their own skills. If we consistently create a homely working atmosphere the children will soon join us, starting by playing near us, and later, perhaps after a few days, beginning to imitate us.

Many of the daily activities in the kindergarten show how this happens. We shall look at sewing and embroidery as an example.

Several times a year a kindergarten teacher will set up a 'sewing corner' for herself during the period of free play for several days at a time. She will have a basket of material or felt which she might use to make simple dolls or dolls' clothes. In another basket she keeps her scissors, a pin cushion, a thimble and different coloured rolls of thread. Luckily she has a children's version of the same things. They join in happily and enthusiastically, depending on their age and temperament. Three- to four-year-olds often choose a larger piece of material from the basket. They 'tackle' this with a pair of scissors, their lips firmly pressed together or their tongue moving in concentration. The longest needle with the largest eye is just right for them. If the needle is threaded with a long piece of thread, by one of the older children or an adult, it will then be pushed through the material, with the whole hand, again and again until the material is crumpled together into a ball. Suddenly we hear a happy cry 'I have made a bird,' as the piece of material, held by the child, flies singing through the room.

A four-year-old boy might accidentally sew a few bits of unspun wool into his crumpled ball. He asks 'May I take my sheep home?' His friend begins by finding the right sized thimble before he too begins to sew, his protected finger extended.

Five-year-olds set to work in quite a different way. A girl might want to sew a little gnome. Carefully she chooses a piece of felt, cuts it to shape and with skilful stitches sews the hood

Baking potatoes in the fire

32

on top just as she has seen adults do. After she has filled the rest of the body with wool and sewn it together at the front she immediately begins a second one. Then she puts both of them in her pocket, kneels on the floor and builds a cave for them with little pieces of wood and stones. Two other children have in the meantime selected the most beautiful buttons from the button box and eagerly sewn them onto a piece of cloth. The teacher is then asked to cut button holes in the opposite side of the material. One of the children now notices that if the button-thread goes over the edge of the button rather than through the button hole in the middle, they do not button so well. Resolutely, she reaches for the scissors and sews the button on once more — this time correctly.

Three and four-year-old children may simply imitate the activity of sewing, taking the material and using their childish imagination to give a name to what they have made only after it has been completed. Five-year-olds, in contrast, are much more purposeful from the start. To a much greater extent they can picture clearly what they want, and given their rich imagination and imitative ability, can enthusiastically translate this into action.

In the last months before they start school children's manual dexterity becomes so much more sophisticated that they are able not only to thread needles, but also to sew 'proper' seams with fine needles. They also take it for granted that a real tailor puts a thimble on the right middle finger. If they are given a large piece of soft material to make their own doll their creativity is given free reign. They might carefully sew on hair woven into long plaits, christening robes, aprons with pockets, bibs, jackets with buttons and all sorts of things. Or they might be happy with embroidered swaddling clothes for their doll. It doesn't matter. There are all sorts of different opportunities, particularly in free play, for the children to practise manual dexterity and perseverance and to develop an overview of what they are making.

Embroidery is another example of a type of 'handwork' which allows children creative freedom. Regularly each year they will see their teacher devoting herself to embroidering aprons which the children are allowed to wear during the period of free play. They can imitate such embroidery as freely as possible by allowing their needle to 'go for a walk' with colourful threads over the material. Some children will select the colours with great care, others reach for them arbitrarily. One might take 'giant steps' with his needle while another 'walks' backwards and forwards but doesn't travel across the material. It is evident from this that sewing and embroidery allow much more creative freedom than, for example, weaving.

The increasingly correct use of tools through imitation introduces the children to normal, meaningful activity in life. Whether this is taken up by children at this age depends on their strength of will, their imitative capacity and not least on the ability of the adults around them to create a happy, industrious atmosphere through their recurring activity.

The ears for the harvest wreath are cut to size

– 4 –

Kindergarten work and the 'mantle' of the child's life forces

To see how the daily activities in the kindergarten can become a 'mantle,' for the life forces of the child, we need to consider, in the first instance, the function or task of a 'mantle.'

On the one hand a mantle should provide protection from external things, but on the other it should enable something to flourish internally, to be ordered, strengthened and tended. Although a mantle is something which sets limits, it does not necessarily close off and it can mediate between the inner and the outer. This function of the mantle can be seen everywhere it develops in a natural way.

If we look at a medieval town, we see that it is surrounded by walls which are broken at intervals by gates. Through these gates we see life — people on foot, on horseback, in carriages — streaming in and out. Next to and above the gates are towers with guards who ensure that nothing is illegally taken in or out and who close the gates in good time when hostile forces approach.

Every other mantle which we might quote — for example, the house with its doors and windows enclosing the children's daily life and play space, clothing, skin which breathes, the physical body with its sensory gateways — is something which mediates between the inside and the outside.

Probably the most comprehensive mantle is formed by warmth, and this applies to all levels. For our physical comfort we ensure we have warm clothes and heated rooms. On another level we attempt to create a soul-warmth, 'an honest, unaffected love ... which as it were streams through the physical environment of the child with warmth [which] may literally be said to "hatch out" the forms of the physical organs.'[4] A mantle of warmth is created on a spiritual level if we allow wisdom to rule our thinking, if our thoughts are fully concentrated on the matter in hand and if our actions are based on knowledge of the human being. Rudolf Steiner often says that love is wanting to do that of which one has gained an understanding.

A mantle of warmth cannot be taken for granted — it needs to be continually recreated. In our efforts to do this we are working with the three basic virtues. These are particularly important in the first three years of childhood but should continue to be cultivated in our educational work until school age. In the first three years they are: lovingly supporting the process of learning to walk; surrounding children with truthfulness as they learn to talk; ensuring that an atmosphere of clarity pervades as children's thinking develops.[5]

In all the examples which follow, we should never lose sight of the specific functions of the mantle of warmth and the three basic virtues, which underline it and are necessary to sustain it.

If we look at some examples from the immediate day-to-day work of the kindergarten we can demonstrate how they can assist in the creation of a mantle of warmth, or how they might counteract such a process.

Let us look first of all at the mantle which is created through our own behaviour, our actions and our attitudes. We shall call it the 'mantle of activity.' Most importantly it should involve the creation of a world worth imitating. Rudolf Steiner says in this context: 'And so the task of a kindergarten teacher is to adjust work taken from daily life so that it becomes suitable for the children's play activities'[6] 'Adjust work' is the key element.

We shall take three examples of such work which is connected to the care and cleanliness of the environment and discover how we can 'adjust work.'

Caring for the environment: housework

At the end of the week, towards the end of the free play period, the 'cleaner' (that is the teacher or the assistant) comes. She has a tin of fragrant polish and cloths for cleaning and polishing. The children then empty the small compartments. The cleaner knocks at the doors or rings the bells of the dolls houses, then carefully wipes the compartments with the polishing cloth and immediately there are eager offers to help polish. While the children put the things back into one compartment, the cleaner moves on to the next one. Sometimes the polishers will accompany the cleaner to the shopping corner and the big toy shelf. This process of cleaning round the whole room introduces the general routine of tidying up.

The second example gives an idea of what might happen in the 'ironing room.' The teacher fetches the ironing board with the iron and brings it into the middle of the room from where the whole room can be observed. Next to the ironing board is a table on which the finished ironing can be carefully stacked. She takes one cloth after another out of the ironing basket, wets it, rolls it up and puts it on a surface which won't be damaged. Then she sits down at the ironing board, takes one role, spreads out the cloth, iron it and puts it neatly folded on the table. The obvious pleasure in this work is clear to the children and it will not take long before a plentiful supply of 'food' and 'drink' will be provided by the children. The 'ironer' is a focus of calmness in the play room and may also become the focus of play.

The third example describes a spring cleaning situation (although I do not mean to give the impression that we do nothing but clean in our kindergarten).

On the appointed day chairs, stools and benches were to be cleaned. A protective covering was put over a table and the tin of polish and the cleaning and polishing cloths were laid out in preparation. The children pushed up all the chairs in the room and placed them in long rows next to one another. I was asked to keep removing the ones at the front so that the whole 'train' could move forward several places. The chairs which had been cleaned were placed in the open doorway, where they were busily polished and then pushed out into the corridor. Before long the chairs turned back into a train or a café or park benches.

Three of our youngest children had decided that on this particular day they needed to use chairs for the walls of their 'house.' I said to them 'Let's polish your chairs and then you'll be able to use freshly polished chairs.' 'Oh yes!' they answered. Soon afterwards they were sitting on the workbench singing Christmas songs with great conviction even though it was Easter time.

Not all children took part in the cleaning activity. Some sat on the corner bench and sewed. A six-year-old boy sat next to them and 'played' a lullaby with great devotion on a stick. A birthday was being celebrated in the dolls' corner. 'Neighbours' built their house next to where the cleaning was going on.

As with all other activities, for example sewing, carving, washing or cooking, we need to set up a 'room' or 'workshop' with all the necessary materials and tools and then happily undertake the work.

So where in these examples do we find the 'forms' which enable the children's experience of daily life and work to flow through the children's activity into new play? And what is needed for such work to turn into a mantle for the children? I suggest they are as follows:

— Creating clear work processes into which the children can be integrated very easily. In accordance with their age, the children may occasionally turn the work into a game but they are still finding their place in the work of adults.

— Thinking through the work in advance and carrying it out in a logical order, up to and including tidying up the work place.

— Working calmly and briskly, though not hectically, without boredom and always with pleasure. Thoughts should be concentrated fully on our own activity as well as being extended over what is happening in the room so that all the children feel that they are being taken care of.

— Persevering in our work over a period of at least several days (with exceptions of course). In this way we repeat our work regularly and do not simply do it when we happen to think of it or spontaneously feel like it.

This inner discipline creates the forms into which we should introduce the work which has to be done in life. All of it invokes calmness and introduces industriousness into play, creating a mantle! The children are left actively in peace — paradoxical as that may sound — and do not constantly need to ask 'What are you doing today' or 'What are we doing now?'

Faulty formation of the mantle

Two of the above examples will now serve to illustrate how the same activities did not lead to the formation of a mantle.

The person doing the ironing had taken the washing from the stand and thought that it was probably not necessary to spray it with water. But when they started ironing, they soon noticed that not all the creases were coming out of the clothes. They bent down to the basket, took two lots of washing and splashed water between them without being aware of the way they were doing it. It looked as if they did not really like ironing; their work did not radiate any pleasure and they gave the impression of being preoccupied rather than being aware of the whole of the room. They had not given sufficient thought either to what was needed to create the right imitative atmosphere for the children or to how they went about things, might affect the rest of the room. Their only concern had been to do as much as possible in the shortest possible time. There was no contact with the children playing in the room.

The same thing happened during spring cleaning. The stands and chairs had been set out for cleaning. After I had finished watering the flowers, had briefly been called to the telephone, welcomed some newly arrived children and had returned to the room, both members of staff were sitting in the dolls house — without being noticed by anybody — and had already cleaned all the stands and stools. They did not at first understand my disappointed reaction because they had wanted to be helpful and were proud to have finished everything so quickly. But they had not allowed time for a joyful creative atmosphere to become established, and they had not created any forms which would have enabled the children to play with enthusiasm. They merely wanted to finish as quickly as possible. Yet the important thing is not that the work should be finished as quickly as possible with minimum effort, but that activities take place in which the children can participate in a meaningful way. It is also important that they can leave these processes but still be immersed in a sense of warm, joyful activity.

If we could manage to be enthusiastic about our daily chores as teachers and parents our children would really be blessed. We need to remember that doing housework is also educational.

Helping overactive and inactive children

What do we do for children who do not allow themselves to be 'enveloped' by processes, who do not become active in the right way by themselves or who have an unhappy relationship with their surroundings? They might be very fidgety or destructive, or particularly inactive, simply sitting around and watching while others move about and work.

Overactive children can find their way into play if the flow of activity is gradually guided into more meaningful paths through consistent guidance.

It is much more difficult to gain access to inactive children and a great deal of tact is required. Initially it is good to leave them in peace, surrounding them with a sense of trust and hope. It is really important that they feel totally comfortable in the well-ordered new surroundings of the children's group and with the new way of doing things. Gradually, we can attempt to make it easier for them to relate to their surroundings by occasionally accompanying small pieces of work with a few words. For example: 'Now let's fetch a broom,' or 'Now we still need the fat wool sack.' We can also occasionally ask them to do something, such as buying a 'roll' at the 'shop' for the 'sewing person' cook lunch and take it to the sewing room, or fetch a 'crying' baby doll so that we can tend to it in the sewing room. If this does not help the child find a way into its own activity it is good to leave it completely in peace again. A sudden change may occur after what might be a considerable interval.

This is what happened to a particular four-year-old boy. He was a very alert child who had been brought up rather intellectually. He had been in kindergarten for nine months, had only watched the adults and had never played. The only thing he eagerly got involved in was tidying up. One day I took my piece of carving from the workbench and sat down on the next-door bench where this boy also happened to be sitting. Suddenly he said: 'all right, you can sit in my boat too.' After a short interval he continued, 'And if you have any dirty washing, just give it to me. I've got a washing machine here.' A large empty basket stood next to him. This was the first time that this boy had expressed his imagination and it was the start of an infinitely rich and fulfilled period of play over the following two years.

A five-year-old boy also gradually established a healthy relationship with his surroundings. He had observed me very attentively on the first day as the ironing lady. On the second day he sat down beside me at the ironing board and involved himself in the work process. When I had folded a cloth, he held his open hands towards me, took the cloth and then laid it on the correct pile. Then he handed me one of the rolled up cloths and waited until it was folded. On the third day he sat down opposite the ironing board and pulled the cloth forward a bit at a time as he had observed me do. What had happened? He had made contact with his surroundings in a meaningful way and felt himself enveloped by the pleasure and gratitude of the

A six-year-old rocks the doll she has made herself in a hammock

adult. This pleasure and gratitude was expressed clearly but was not over-emphasized as this would have separated him from the contact he had just established and would have set him apart from his activity.

Rhythmical structuring of time and dealing with interruptions

We shall now give examples of a second 'mantle' which arises through the rhythmical structuring of time. All children experience two great 'breaths' in their day at the kindergarten. The first great 'breathing out phase,' during which they can more or less follow their own inclinations, consists of the period of free play plus tidying up and going to the washroom. Then there is a short 'breathing in phase' during the rhythmical games and morning snack, when all the children become bound up with what the group is doing. After the snack a second 'breathing out period' consists of free play in the garden or during the walk. The conclusion of the morning — usually a fairy tale — again forms a brief 'breathing in period.'

The rhythmic structure remains the same every day. It becomes a good habit, a mantle. Everyone knows how disruptive it can be for children when time is treated in an arbitrary fashion. If a father, for example, comes to collect his child early simply because he has finished at work, the child may be quite disorientated.

Life often throws unexpected events at us and they can be naturally integrated into our routines. For example, rather than sending away a mother who knocks and wants to register her child for kindergarten because we do not want to be disturbed at this particular moment we can quickly arrange another time for a meeting with her. We do not make the delivery man with a large parcel wait until we have finished the rhythmical games which we happen to be playing before signing for it. Such 'disruptions' can be accommodated within the regulated course of the day and generally the children can rely on today being like yesterday and tomorrow.

Such order and security enveloped the souls of the children before they were born and left the divine world of the Father. Here on earth they should be enabled to create a link with their pre-birth experiences and to rediscover what is familiar to them. We need to allow something of the light of the realm before birth to illuminate our deeds and the way we conduct ourselves, so that our children are accompanied securely into their new life. The 'time mantle' also becomes the 'mantle of habit.' The more we create the conditions for good, active habits in the children, the more these habits become a mantle and the less we shall need disciplinary words.

Habit formation makes punishment superfluous

This can be demonstrated by using the examples of the two transition periods during the morning, which can be critical and chaotic. Firstly, the transition from free play to breakfast. It is a good idea to begin tidying up by means of an activity rather than with an acoustic signal such as a bell or a song for example. After all, tidying up should also happen through imitation. Initially the adult tidies up their work area and then starts trying to create 'rough' order in the room — in approximately the same sequence each day and with the assistance of the older children — by putting the furniture back in its place. Then everything can to be picked up off the floor and the various

Above: Point of calmness during spring cleaning: six-year-olds in front of their 'music stands' making music for their doll children.

Opposite: Washing clothes, which can be done outside when the weather is warm enough

corners can carefully be tidied up. Even the youngest children may now become aware that this is the tidying up period and they may join in their own way. Soon they are allowed to go to the washroom. Others follow, finishing with the ones responsible for folding the cloths and tidying them up. On returning there is plenty of work for everyone. A table cloth is placed in the middle of each table, place mats and spoons need to be laid and a vase of flowers put on each table. The side table with cutlery and bowls is prepared. All the children have now returned from the washroom and sit in their seats. The group leader too sits down and looks around at everyone once more. Then she stands up, perhaps saying the words 'Let's set to work' and straight away begins with rhythmical play. Afterwards, when all children are back in their seats, she distributes the food. Then she also sits down, folds her hands and says 'We are ready' and waits a moment until everyone is quiet. This is followed by grace.

Children need to absorb new routines, so it will only be possible to structure the transition period in this way after a careful and patient accustomization period. At the beginning the adult goes to the washroom together with the children, helping to establish good habits by visiting the toilet and then washing hands, using water, soap and a towel. Everyone waits on the cloakroom bench until the adult sits down as well. They might then do a little action dance as they make their way back to the table. The adult then makes sure that everyone finds their place at the breakfast table, as that provides a sense of security, a mantle, and prevents any discussion as to who wants to or does not want to sit next to whom, at which table and so on.

Such habits very quickly establish themselves in children and one can quickly move on to the more relaxed form of transition period described earlier. The aim in all cases should be to organize as little as possible and to regulate daily life as much as possible through real, meaningful activity. One will then not be forced to keep the children happy with little games at all sorts of appropriate or inappropriate times. Instead, children who are guided by the rhythms and actions of everyday life quickly become well-balanced and are eager and happy to help.

The second transition period occurs during the changeover from playing in the garden or going for a walk to listening to the fairy tale. All the toys are carried back inside, the children empty the sand in their shoes into the little bucket in the corridor, put on their indoor shoes and wash their hands. Then anyone who wants to may fetch a baby doll and dress it in the fairy tale corner until everyone arrives. The adult sits down in her seat, she looks around the group, cleans a nose here or there and ties any outstanding bows on the dolls. As she does this, the adult drops her voice considerably in order to create a greater degree of calmness. Then she begins 'Once upon a time ...'

In the winter, when lots of outdoor clothes need to be shed, we might recite a little verse 'Hat comes first, then coat and shoe — and quietly too.' This ensures that the children untie their shoelaces properly, rather than sliding them off and flinging them away.

Everything which we develop in this way over time takes on the function of form and ritual and thus becomes a mantle. We have to take care, of course, that form does not become excessive, that there is always sufficient breathing space in all that we do and that the children are able to live with us in the same way that a mother lives with her children. We need to constantly observe our actions — even our minor ones — and strive to measure them against our understanding of the human being.

The railway made of footstools

Using language in the right way

The last 'mantle' which we shall describe is the one which arises through our use of words.

In the context of play we do not need to use many words. A purposeful sentence to encourage play or a further stage of play is often sufficient. The important thing is that it should lead directly to activity. On one occasion two five-year-olds had built themselves a doctor's surgery and had lovingly furnished it. Suddenly they came to me and said with some disappointment 'No one wants to be our patient.' Instead of encouraging other children to go to the surgery, or going there myself, I simply stuck out my foot and said 'This needs some ointment, and some bandages.' The children saw to this, and even brought medicine in the form of 'drops' and 'pills' and hot tea. Immediately there was great interest in my injured foot causing many others to want to be patients so that the waiting room was full.

We also need words when danger looms. For example, two chairs on a table move too close to the edge. Or a swimming bath is built, and a diving board is added. In such situations it is always better to say how things should be done rather than how they should not be done. If we give positive advice, the activity can continue, whereas if we say what the children should not do they are faced with a hiatus, left to their own devices and have to have new ideas themselves. The mantle disappears for a moment because the adult did not follow the golden rule which says: don't forbid without offering an alternative! (This does not mean that there will not be occasions on which one has to say forcefully 'That's enough!')

It is also important to protect children from concepts and ideas which are too sharply defined. For example, when a five year old wants to know about the birth of babies, a few hints about the origin in heaven of the human soul and the mediating role of the guardian angel are quite sufficient and appropriate for the time being. There is no need at this stage for a clinical description of how babies are created in the womb.

Sharply defined concepts or truth-filled images?

We learn from Rudolf Steiner that during their first seven years children will be more able to encounter the reality of the spiritual world as they sleep if they have not been bombarded with specific concepts and ideas. 'That is why children often acquire a certain awareness of spiritual reality from sleep ... Sharply defined concepts cloud the view of the spiritual realities surrounding the child between the time of going to sleep and waking up.'[7] This comes to an end roughly at the time when, around the age of seven, children lose their first teeth and gain their adult ones. At this stage of development the forces which built the body are now liberated from it and are themselves sent into sleep.

There are still wonderful moments when we feel that we have been inspired with the right ideas or answers for children, and that these inspirations were not of our making. During Advent, the weeks leading up to Christmas, the children live with the story of St Nicholas and his helpers, who in our house are responsible for all the mysterious things which happen in this time. In the Christmas holidays, a six-and-a-half-year-old girl once asked me 'Do *you* make the shepherds in the nativity garden move forward or do St Nicholas' helpers do it?' I replied, 'We always keep very quiet about secrets like that.' Some time later she came back and asked: 'And what about the chain of nuts? Do you make that as well?' I replied 'That is another one of those secrets.' She went off again, quite satisfied, but returned a third time to ask 'But what about the basket of surprises? Do you do that as well, or is that really done by the helpers?' (The basket of surprises is brought by St Nicholas, and every day it contains a little surprise item from nature with which the children can decorate their own moss garden.) After the emphasis of her question I felt I really had to answer her properly, otherwise she would have been very disappointed. So I answered, 'That is really done by the helpers. But did you know that everyone can be a helper. All adults can be helpers and all children can become helpers.'

If we can answer children's questions more and more with clear images and a truthfulness which becomes evident over time, we shall create protective mantles for the children and allow their life forces to flourish.

Conclusion

To finish looking at how the work in the kindergarten forms a protective mantle we should consider what we can do in order to turn this mantle into a foundation for the whole of the child's later life?

We have to protect and nurture the physical mantle of the child in the same way as a mother provides a physical mantle to her unborn child. Again and again Rudolf Steiner reminds us that we can offer the right kind of support to the body in its task of forming the physical organs.[8]

This means, for example, that 'what the forces and fluids of the enveloping [mantle of the] mother ... have done for [the physical body] hitherto, must from now onward be done for it by the forces and elements of the external physical world. ... the physical organs must *mould themselves into definite shapes.*

Their whole structural nature must receive *certain tendencies and directions.* ... It is the right physical environment alone, which works upon the child in such a way that the physical organs *shape themselves aright.* ... in the process of imitation [the child's] physical organs *are cast into the forms* which then become permanent.'

Moralizing and instructing do not have the appropriate effect in a child. 'Rather it is what the grown-up people do visibly before his eyes. ... The child, however, does not learn by instruction or admonition, but by imitation. The physical organs *shape their forms* through the influence of the physical environment ... If the child sees only foolish actions in his surroundings, the brain *will assume such forms* as adapt it also to foolishness in later life.'

As we have seen in the sections dealing with toys and dolls, there is an emphasis on simplicity so that the powerful and strengthening force of the imagination is given as much scope as possible. 'The work of the imagination *moulds and builds the forms* of the brain.' A good example of this is a toy which has two figures mounted on two movable blocks. The two figures take it in turns to hammer. There are also picture books in which individual figures are moved when threads are pulled, so that action is introduced into an otherwise still picture. 'All this brings about a living mobility of the organs, and by such mobility *the right forms of the organs* are built up.'

There is also emphasis on joy and pleasure, when Rudolf Steiner describes how teachers should encourage a healthy desire and sense of striving to arise in children. 'Pleasure and delight are the forces which most rightly *quicken and call forth the physical forms* of the organs.'

I would like to close this chapter with a passage which has already been referred to. 'Thus the joy of the child, in and with his environment, must be reckoned among the forces that *build and mould* the physical organs. Teachers [are needed] with a happy look and manner, and above all with an honest and unaffected love. A love which as it were streams through the physical environment of the child with warmth may literally be said to *"hatch out" the forms* of the physical organs.'

All these elements are part of the 'right physical environment' of the children and they exist in the place for which we are responsible. Our activity, along with the comfort of physical warmth and a warmth of the soul and of the spirit, should turn this place into the appropriate physical environment for children in the years following birth, forming a protective mantle for their life forces.

− 5 −

Setting an example and educating the will

We shall now look at the development and education of the will — mainly in the final stages of the pre-school period. We shall also see how this is reflected in adults and in the example they provide. Adults face a challenge of will in their strength, their inner and outer self-assurance, their consistency in loving, their happiness and humour, the scope of their imagination, their alertness and so on. This challenge is particularly evident when they are called upon to be aware of and deal with the sensitive moments which occur during the transitional phases of education.

We shall start by outlining the early stages of child development since these have a decisive influence on the period between five and seven years of age.

At the start of their lives small children display a great openness which is at the mercy of all the influences of their environment. Small children are like eyes which just allow impressions to enter and pass through. The eyes themselves are selflessly at the disposal of the person looking through them. It is the observer who needs the element of will to actually see something. The whole physical body serves as the sensory organ of the soul and spirit of the human being.

'There is little that has a more wonderful effect upon the human heart than to see how from day to day, week to week, month to month, year to year, in the first period of childhood the inner spirit and soul elements are breaking forth, to see how from the chaotic movements of the limbs, from the glance absorbed by outer things, from the play of expressions which we feel do not as yet really belong to the child, there develops and impresses itself on the surface of the human form all that proceeds from the centre, from the middle point of man, where the divine-spiritual being descending from pre-earthly life is unfolding itself.'[9] We are thus dealing with two phenomena:

1. Children exist wholly in the senses.
2. Children exist wholly in the will.

The will is used to take hold of and assimilate the world through the senses. The synthesis and the interaction of these two phenomena becomes evident in the power of imitation which the child brings with it from before birth. Imitation represents the dual process of reception through the senses and subsequent reproduction through the will.

Rudolf Steiner wrote: 'By a right application of the fundamental educational principles during the first seven years of childhood the foundation is laid for the development of a strong and healthy *Will.* For a strong and healthy will must have its support in the well-developed forms of the physical body.'[10]

The organs of small children do not yet possess their characteristic forms and have not yet found their individual rhythms. Small children are the most unrhythmical beings we know.

This leads to the questions: How do the individual organs receive their characteristics and rhythms, and how does their rhythmical interaction as an organism arise? How does the structure and purposeful expression of the will come about?

The answer is, mainly through external influences. Children need to be embedded in rhythmical patterns, for instance in their repetitive activities such as waking, sleeping and eating. Children, as creatures of the will and the senses, nestle into their environment whatever it may be. Their organs are moulded and they learn to order their will.

Environment and the will of small children

We shall look briefly at the period up to the age of three. Apart from the tremendous effort of will in acquiring upright posture, walking and speech, children have a wealth of opportunities to practise their will unconsciously, for example in grasping things, letting go, throwing things, manipulating a spoon, using a mug, dressing themselves, eagerly following their parents doing household chores, unpacking the shopping, preparing meals. These are all activities which practise skills and in which the will acquires a sense of purpose. The limbs no longer flail around chaotically; there is purposeful activity. Nevertheless, children learn to move about in their environment with increasing security not by reflecting on what they are doing but by imitating.

If every learning stage is to be accompanied by love and pleasure at this age, it must also include a sensitive drawing of boundaries. After all, children do not simply imitate, they also explore. If they begin, for example, spreading spinach all over the table, tugging at the tablecloth or the flex of the iron, clumsily spilling their drinks or knocking over the wastepaper basket as they run past, and are laughed at followed around to see what they will get up to next, bad habits will be created. But these can be avoided if the adult thinks ahead, imaginatively distracts the child and acts consistently; in other words, creates an environment of security and guidance. The important thing is always to guide children's will while they are still incapable of doing so.

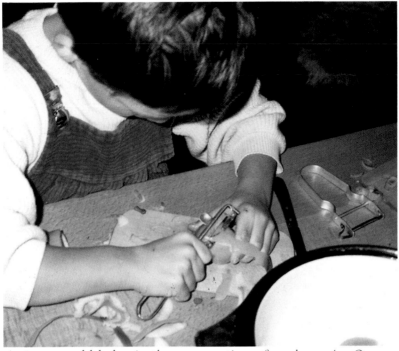

A six-year-old helps in the preparation of apple purée. Occa-sionally he succeeds in peeling of a strip which is just as long and snail-like as the adult's one.

One of the first obvious crises comes when children learn to say 'no' as well as 'I.' Their own will begins to emerge to a greater of lesser degree. In the first instance the will simply expresses itself, but then it gradually has to learn to blend harmoniously with the demands of the immediate environment. It is a great help if good habits have already been established, and if there is already a rhythmical structure to the day, with thoughtfulness in the way things are done, and care and good manners at meal-times and in the preparation of food.

The will and dawning imagination

The age of three sees the release of the formative life forces which are mainly responsible for the work of the head in the formation of the main organs of the body. These now work together with the formative forces which are gradually liberating themselves from the organs in the middle sphere of the child's body. New abilities become evident in the child's development. If up to this point the child's will was directed mainly at objects used by the parents around the house, it now begins to work more and more with the developing imagination, growing in strength all the time. Imagination allows us to move beyond what surrounds us into the boundless realm of possibility. The will present in the imagination is able to accept as real what might only faintly resemble reality; with innate joy and power it turns reality into what it wants it to be, using it to create something new. For example, in the middle of shoe cleaning, the mundane sight of the shoes being cleaned can suddenly inspire the child to see the shoe brush as a ship or an aeroplane. Or a mother might have wrapped a parcel and hung the rest of the string over the back of a chair. Her child is reminded of a crane and ties a wooden spoon to one end of the string, slowly pulling it up by the other end.

So memory and recollection work simultaneously with the imagination. But memory can only offer us what we have already experienced. The imagination can recreate our experiences and observations straight away if it can focus on something similar to what we have already seen. The power of the will lights up in the imagination and the memory, turning it into action.

There are certainly children who do not take hold of their imagination with their will and who may behave erratically if they are not properly guided. For example, they will race around imitating engines, behave wildly in unfamiliar surroundings and be destructive. Or they may be completely inactive within themselves, lacking in drive and energy, for example occupying themselves for hours with the way a tricycle works.

It is possible to distinguish between *harmoniously* active children, *erratically* or aimlessly active children, and children in whom the will is inhibited, or even paralysed. For example, 'harmonious' children might use an old cloth for dressing up or for building a house. The unpredictably active ones would throw it on the ground or slide across the floor on it, knocking over a vase of flowers.

If the will develops in a healthy way, children around three to five years of age will constantly develop new ideas as they play. For instance, two four-year-old-girls placed all the chairs they could find in rows of two, laid all their dolls and finally themselves on the chairs and said 'this is our sleeper train.' Then they placed the rows of chairs opposite one another, put all the dolls on one row and said 'now it's a baby changing table.' Soon afterwards they arranged all the chairs so that their backs faced each other and spread a large cloth over them to build a puppet theatre. A footstool became a motorbike, then a

doll's birthday table, then a letter box and finally, with other footstools piled on top of it, a waterfall with chestnuts cascading from one to another.

The crisis of will and imagination around the age of five

At around the age of five an obvious crisis can be observed in many children, particularly in those who are actively creative. Further changes occur in children's development because the formative forces actively structuring the body from within are increasingly freeing themselves from the metabolic and limb system. The will has to re-orientate itself to unite with the ideas which are gradually awakening in children of this age. This takes a while. For a time children will not have so many imaginative ideas, their will appears to be paralysed and they ask 'What shall I do?' or say: 'I'm bored.' We should not appeal to the imagination at this point as it needs to be treated with care and should be left in peace. We can let the children do small, straightforward activities which they will see as being related to what adults do. For example:
— cutting out, sewing, drawing small picture books;
— making needle cases, arranging needles into them;
— sandpapering a letter opener which has been quickly carved by an adult;
— *requesting* help, *without making demands!*
— threading a ribbon or a piece of elastic;
— drying up, sweeping;
— sawing wood in the garden place

This kind of work should take place near an adult as the

Six-year-old in the boat he has built himself.

children want and need such proximity. They are still going through a period of imitation even if they are genuinely beginning to work. For the first time there is a hint of obligation but entirely within the context of imitative activity. After a certain period of 'work' they will want to play again. The imagination recalls pictures of real life situations for example a hairdresser, a hospital with an ambulance, a fishing boat, a shop, a family, a fire brigade, a space ship and turns them into impulses for play.

The will unites with the power of ideas

It is important to remember that while the environment and the toys have not changed, the relationship to them has. If the will wants to act on an impulse to play, it must now unite with the idea. With the aid of the imagination, which has been so richly practised in the past, it finds or transforms objects into what the idea demands. This is a key process.

Imagination, patience, perseverance and enthusiasm are all necessary in order to put an idea for play into practice, as is the readiness to overcome problems. The will is strongly involved in all these qualities but in a way which is determined by the activities.

For example a child under the age of five might see a bent stick, pick it up and say 'I'm a chimney sweep.' After the age of five the child first has the idea of wanting to be a chimney sweep and then says: 'To be a chimney sweep I need a long rolled up brush.' The child looks for one and finally makes one by tying a feather duster to a long piece of string and then fixing the string to a stick.

Before the age of five the will took hold of an object which, — after an external prompt, took on life in the imagination.

Now the will has to work from within itself to establish a purposeful connection between the idea and the imagination. Children who have plenty of opportunities to practise this kind of internal work are lucky! It requires effort and may be difficult. However, if the objective is achieved it is cause for deep satisfaction or even noisy celebration.

If children are not given any opportunity for this kind of internal work they can easily become unruly. This makes us think that they should be put to work — for example sandpapering, sawing, nailing — and that they simply need to perform some strenuous task in which they can really work their muscles. They certainly should be allowed to do this, when it is required in the normal course of events. An attentive and forward thinking educator will find enough opportunities for this throughout the year, for example

— sawing up branches left in the garden after the trees have been pruned in late winter;
— renewing the borders of flower beds and moving large stones in the summer;
— attaching logs to boards in the garden to make steam rollers;
— excavating lakes and rivers with a spade;
— playing games involving running, calling, catching, rolling tyres, skipping.

These are all important activities and children and teachers may work or play in this way with great enthusiasm. However, we should not forget that the forces of the will should not only be practised in physical activity but also, particularly at this age, internally, in the handling of living ideas. If children grow strong in this sphere as well, they are more likely to become balanced individuals. Nevertheless, if children do not have the opportunity to exercise their imagination it is better for them to engage in physical work rather that to go racing wildly around.

Assistance from adults in purposeful play

At the time when children begin to play purposefully, they are often still dependent on help from an adult. The inner 'accompaniment,' the empathy, the imagination and restrained enthusiasm of adults are vital for them. For example a six-year-old boy pretended to be a circus ringmaster. He dressed several children with different pieces of cloth to transform them into specific animals, he made 'cages' for them and told them what they were to do in the show. For quite a while all of them tacitly did what he said. But eventually play began to stagnate, ideas ran out and the fun disappeared. Help was required. I said that now that the circus had finished it was time for the circus folk to have a snack. The lad answered 'Yes and then they will pack everything up and drive to another town. Here's my van,' indicating a table with supports. 'Circus vans have a round roof like this one, don't they?' The table had just been serving as an animal cage and it was right next to my work table. He worked a bit more to improve the van and then looked out through the window by my work table and said 'Oh, I'm at the border already! Now we're entering another country with a lot of snow. I'll need a snow plough.'

With great effort he tied a wooden shovel to the front of the van to act as a snow-plough. He arranged gritting equipment at the back of the van by piling stools on top of one another and letting chestnuts drop through the handholds. The next day, this lad built another van (without a snow-plough and salting equipment) and said 'Now it's a train engine.' He added chairs and tables to make carriages, and other children joined in, but no real play developed. I intervened again and said: 'You've got a luggage van. As I've got to go on a trip your porters could collect my luggage. And you've got a dining car so the

Six-year-olds sawing wood

travellers can eat on their journey.' A great deal of activity ensued. Luggage (big pieces of wood) was fetched and loaded into the van, the dining car was built and furnished. This time I did not need to leave my seat as I was incorporated into the game where I was. I was given the menu and then the most magnificent dishes and no one thought twice about the fact that I was not sitting in the 'real' dining car, although I certainly will do on other occasions.

Another lad had built a camp with his friends but no play ensued under a table. I suggested, 'Shouldn't a camp site have a fire where we can cook meals?' 'Oh yes. Can we have some sticks?' 'Yes, go and fetch three.' With difficulty they tied the sticks together to make a tripod, built a fire underneath it with red and yellow pieces of cloth and blocks of wood and hung a basket with a handle in the middle to act as a cooking pot. They asked for another two sticks which they placed across two chair backs, covering them with cloth to make tents. They furnished them with rugs, cushions and small stools. By the time they had finished doing all of this it was time to tidy up, though the boys complained that they had not yet started to play!

In the final year of kindergarten another crisis in the way children play may occur, particularly at the time when the school is interviewing prospective new pupils. The existing children suddenly no longer feel themselves to be kindergarten children and say 'From now on we only want to work!' Children who feel this can be included in the work of the adult and allowed to help properly. After a short time they will begin to play again.

The adult as role model

We have to consider what is necessary in the setting up of a role model so that the will in the children can develop at all the appropriate stages and levels, as described in the play situations.

If, as we have seen (page 59) the organs which are the support of the will, are shaped from outside the developing child, it is necessary for the child's environment to be one of orderliness, rhythm, good habits and loving consistency.

In order to create order, adults always have to think ahead. This will give meaning and order to what they do. It will mean that they are not constantly running about having forgotten something. Thinking ahead also helps to cure bad expressions of will in children.

If for example children are getting into the habit of kicking off their shoes and not taking them off properly with their hands, or if they slam doors, the adult should stand next to them for a moment before they do the offending action, until the habit has been transformed. Adults therefore need to be aware and to anticipate when these moments will occur.

It is also helpful if the adults begin their work in advance. When the children arrive they find a teacher who is already at work. The will of each child settles imitatively into the mood of work even if it turns to something quite different from what the teacher is doing.

A third benefit for the teacher lies in developing a rhythmical structure to the day, perhaps even to the year, basing this on insight into what is appropriate to the children, so that there is regular repetition without everything becoming dry or pedantic.

These, together with a number of other steps, help to create the 'right physical environment,' referred to at the end of the previous chapter (page 57) in which the children can bring

A five-year-old drives the train which he has assembled on a piece of cloth folded lengthways.

order into their will through their ability to imitate and follow the role model and in which they learn to use their will purposefully.

Imitation is the activity of the will. The activity of the will is the activity of the 'I.'

The will is something which belongs to the most personal part of the human being. This can be observed in the way children imitate. All of them have the same model but their reactions are quite different. They range from revealing exactly what the model displayed to appearing hardly to be affected by it at all. The greatest freedom lies in imitation! If educators really work on themselves, checking the role model they are setting up, then children will find what they are unconsciously seeking to enable them to develop their will.

The best basis for the gradual transition from 'want' to 'must' after the age of five lies in the establishment of

— good habits,
— rhythmically recurring periods of activity,
— the preparation and celebration of festivals,
— loving consistency.

All of these have a direct effect on the developing will. It is not a question of giving children orders, or making them do whatever happens to occur to us, but of them wanting to do what they ought to be doing. The time spent in close relation with adults during the preceding period of education lays the foundation for this.

Even though we can now use words more and more to help form ideas, telling children what they ought to be doing or how they should be doing it, or using encouraging words to strengthen their perseverance or patience, imitation is still the most important skill children have at their disposal.

The example of adults and a sense of duty

Children experience what they ought to be doing by the example set by the adults around them. Children follow this example by imitating it according to their level of maturity.

If, for instance, adults act conscientiously in doing their duties rather than spending too much time in self-indulgence — then this good example will influence the child.

Adults can demonstrate a sense of purpose and perseverance in their work. For example they might make lots of things for a festival or a fair. Or they might take a long time over a piece of carving or embroidery. The children will be exposed to perseverance and care, and will follow the process with interest.

A sense of 'work ethic' can be imparted to a child by our persevering with a task and endeavouring always to find pleasure in our work.

Indirect imitation, in other words, imitating something which has been described or explained, is particularly helpful in developing a sense of 'duty.' It might consist of giving the children vivid descriptions of specific people and what their work involves. The children are able to use these descriptions to develop their ideas and can then transform them into action finding their direction through imitation.

The story of Ludwig the servant is a good example. He always waited on the guests, fetching everything they needed from the kitchen and the cellar. But he was only ever allowed to come as far as the doorway. The lady of the house then took the things from him and brought them to the guests. Immediately after hearing the story of Ludwig the servant, a six-year-old boy was requested to distribute the cups to the children. He took one look at the whole tray and having identified the fullest cup placed it in front of himself with a look of great satisfaction. His eyes then met mine and I said 'Ludwig would not have done that; he always served the others first and himself last.' 'Really?' said the boy, and he took the cup in front of him, put it in front of his neighbour and took the last one for himself.

The master embroiderer is another example: 'He always chooses the most beautiful threads and then simply goes for a walk with the needle; he never embroiders houses or trains.'

Or: A real tailor
is cheerful and nimble,
and puts on his middle finger
a thimble.

The things which the children 'ought' to do and want to do might also include work which is really part of the later school curriculum and which they always look forward to. It is not just the work itself which challenges the children to act as they ought, as they are free to choose what they want to do, but the sense of 'ought' is experienced within the various stages of work.

We allow children to make simple dolls, knotted from a cloth, with a few spots of ink for the face. After a few swaddling clothes are embroidered the baby doll is 'born' and elaborately dressed in whatever way the child wishes.

A sense of 'ought' also means that children have to respond to admonitions. In doing this they have to learn to transform ideas created by words into actions. Before the age of five, the best way of preventing children from doing something is to distract them or guide their attention on to something else. Once children reach five it is appropriate to set clear limits in words. For example, if children are mimicking shooting we can say, 'We do not shoot. I don't like that. That is not what we do.' The words contain all the weight of conviction and the consistency of attitude. The teacher is the authority appropriate to this

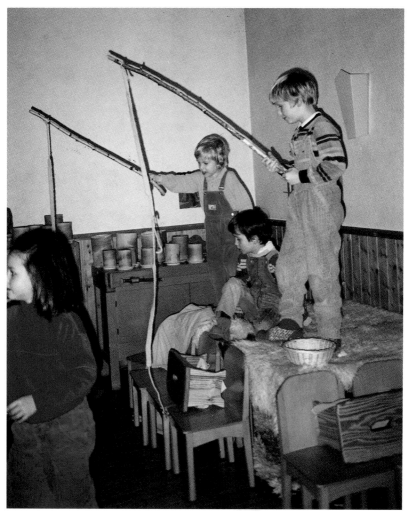

Anglers on their boat wait patiently for a bite, which other children tie to their line on the floor (mostly little woollen sheep or rolled up pieces of cloth).

age, loved and respected, supplementing every prohibition with a positive proposition.

The guiding thoughts behind all that I have attempted to describe are based on the following words by Rudolf Steiner. He says that life up to the age of seven is tied to 'the internally developing will which at this age is not guided by thoughts but by imitating the people encountered by the child.'[11]

The conscious development of the will at school age

The conscious development of the will begins gradually as children reach school age. At this point the teacher distributes tasks such as watering the flowers, wiping the window sills and cleaning the board. These tasks then have to be carried out every day for a week at a time, with the children making an effort even if they do not feel like it. Parents and teachers obviously need to keep the tasks in mind as well, and they may need to remind the children of them. Such help is absolutely vital.

In my view it is too early to expect children to do regular tasks such as these in the kindergarten. (It is much more difficult to be constantly aware of who might be able to do something at any given moment rather than simply making a list!) In any case, there are always regular tasks which are usually done as a rule by adults but which can also be done by the children; such as laying the table, putting flowers in vases, tidying the shoes, distributing the mail, sweeping up, and so on. In some ways it does not matter who does these tasks. Children will always come and ask 'May I ... today?' 'Shall I ... for you?' 'Today I want to because I have never ...'

If a request for help is met with: 'But I don't want to' or 'I don't feel like it' and other children run up and ask: 'May I then?' the teacher has to decide quickly what should be done. Perhaps the request was asking too much of the child concerned. Or perhaps the child is a bit lazy. There are certainly situations in which we have to persist in asking a six-year-old to do something because there are reasons for doing so rather than simply because we think they jolly well ought to!

In these kind of situations and many others we have to lead the children with great sensitivity from imitation to the sought after and beloved figure of authority and we see the extent to which education is truly a high art. We can also see how important the personality of the educator is in relation to the child's imitative activity and therefore to the development of its will.

Notes

1. Freya Jaffke, *Toymaking with Children*, Floris Books, Edinburgh 1988.
2. Rudolf Steiner, *The Education of the Child in the Light of Anthroposophy*, Rudolf Steiner Press, London and Anthroposophic Press, New York, 1981. p. 26.
3. Steiner, *The Education of the Child*, p. 25.
4. Steiner, *The Education of the Child*, p. 28.
5. Rudolf Steiner, *A Modern Art of Education*, Rudolf Steiner Press, London 1981. Lecture 6, 10 August 1923.
6. Rudolf Steiner, *The Child's Changing Consciousness and Waldorf Education*, Anthroposophic Press, New York and Rudolf Steiner Press, London, 1988. Lecture 4, April 18, 1923. p. 81.
7. Rudolf Steiner, *Menschenwerden, Weltenseele und Weltengeist*, (Complete Works Vol. 206), Dornach 1991. Lecture of August 7, 1921.
8. Steiner, *The Education of the Child*, pp.23f, 25, 26, 26f, 28, 28.
9. Rudolf Steiner, *The Essentials of Education*, Rudolf Steiner Press, London 1982. Lecture 2, April 9, 1924. p. 39f.
10. Steiner, *The Education of the Child*, p. 41.
11. Steiner, *The Child's Changing Consciousness*. Lecture 5, April 19, 1923.

Much of the background to the first chapter is inspired by:
Rudolf Steiner, *Soul Economy and Waldorf Education*, Anthroposophic Press, New York 1986.